# Poems by Stan

## Stan Ausberry

A publication of

Eber & Wein Publishing

Pennsylvania

# Poems by Stan

Library of Congress
Cataloging in Publication Data

ISBN 978-1-60880-679-9

Proudly manufactured in the United States of America by

Eber & Wein Publishing

Pennsylvania

*Dedicated to God*
*Almighty in the flesh*
*When He returns to take us home*

*Thank you, Viola*

SAT July 4TH, 2020

DAD

## Foreword

Hopefully a poem for everyone
These are surely the days the Lord has made
From here to eternity
From eternity to here
May God bless you through these words and poems

## Lord's Day

Blessings come from above
Blessings come from love

Reach out to touch the Lord
Reach out to be so kind

Lift me to our level, Lord
Lift me to Your forever

Great is this time
Great is my Lord and mine

## Write

Talk with the pen
Talk with a bend

Grin when you are sad
Grin that triumph smile

We write, we love
We write, we live

Thank you this way
Thank you this day

## To Serve

Be thankful for everything
Grace for another day
Grace for this time
Love from person to person
Love from mine own
Lord bless my soul
Lord bless AL-though
Time will tell you see
Time will tell to be
Thank you over and over
Thank you soldier to soldier

## Polls

When you ask me why
When you do not want to lie

Did you work the polls
Or did you walk too slow

No I don't want to lie
No I will not subside

Blessed is the man who applies
Blessed is the woman who will not cry

I did my part, Lord
I did my part forevermore

# Faith

Write your little heart out
Write with a start

A journal is what we need
A journal is what we see

Pastor set the mark
Pastor upset the cart

Pick up that cross and march
Pick up that cross apart

Life will go on forever
Life is our endeavor

# Country

We are country folk
We are country stock

We lift up our voices
We lift up our courses

Why must we die
Why must we comply

We are country folk
We are not a joke

## Brave

We lift up our voices
We lift up our savior

Be not be dismayed
Be God's friend today

From here and there
From there and here

Lift me up this day
Lift me up, dear Lord, away

# War

Take not my child
Take not my while

The day has come
The day to shun

We are the best
We have request

Lift up my Lord
Lift up His sword

# Christ

Today we celebrate Your birth
Today is great to unearth

Once you reach this age
Once you live away

Beyond the vail
Beyond the pain

There Christ will prevail
There Christ will bless

Lord, thanks for this day
Lord, thanks all the way

## "Please"

Come close to me, my love
Come close to me this fall

Lift up your voice to me
Lift up my voice and say

Please—don't leave me
Please—say you will

Wander over here, my dear
Wander over here no fear

## Love

In the Dale will we
In the Dale with me

Love is what we want
Love is what you have

Honey you are
Honey we shall

In the Dale with me
In the Dale are we

## Lead

Free press is where it's at
Free press will help us lead

One on one is the name of the game
One on one will place us from shame

Leading is a sacred trust
Leading will be a must

## Say

Say it very loud
God has made me well
Say it loud—love abounds
Wait for a while
Wait for a while
God has made me well
God will save my soul
He will save me well
Now and then no more

## Trust

Remember who fed the crowd
Remember who parted the sea

Love me more and more
Love me through and through

Faith in what God can do
Faith and He is able

God has my trust, you see
God has bled and died

And death will pass you by

## President

You can be what you want
You can be in charge

Help me now, oh God
Help me now, King Jesus

Lift up all my faith
Lift up all my faith and grace

Thank you, God
Thank you forever

Now that I am king
Now I show you pleasant things

# Bishop

Teach me what I need to know
Teach me what I need

Jesus is all by my side
Jesus is what I need

Hear me tonight, Lord
Hear me tonight, dear God

You have granted my wish
Wish with Your grace Lordship
Wish with bread and fish

## Dreams

In God's world is my faith
In God's world is my reality

Thank you, Bishop, this night
Thank you, Bishop, for your might

# Do It

Turn a sinner into a saint
Turn me all around the world

Jesus thank you God
Jesus thank you Lord

The words of my mouth
Can save my soul

The words of my mouth
Can give me all the world

Lord, bless your people, sure
Be with me on this
People be blessed—not missed

## Mountain

Move it out of my way
Move it out of my stay

Bring the joy to the valley
Bring the joy from the alley

Yes it was—yes it is

Tears of joy, my Lord
Tears of joy, my God

You have made me the best
You have made me this quest

## Hands

Hang on to God's hand
Praises send to God
Find that tongue
Find that song
Bless me tonight, Lord
Bless me alright
Lose the things of the past
Live with your hands up at last
Live with your life; 'nuff said

## Poetry

My life is the Lord's
My poems are for Him
Moses was great because of God
David was great because of God's love

## You

You make my days so good
You make my coffee just right

When God made you so fine
When God made the sunshine

He looked up my name
He also looked at my pain

Saying, love is what you need
Saying, I'll reach down you see

And giving you to me!

## "Picture Perfect"

Look to each page and smile
Look to the book and grin

Pictures of Vi and me
Pictures of the way we be

The way we hold our hands
The way we close our eyes

Stand straight and erect
Stand straight and be direct

Bless us, Lord, this day
Bless us, Lord, Your way

## Thank You

Grateful are we, you know
Grateful are our souls

Pastor was right on que
Pastor sounded, the words too

Thank you this-a-way
Thank you among all these

My love grows so strong
My love is a grateful heart

Thank you for the start
Thank you, Lord, and never be apart

## Come Close

Be with me if you can
Be with me for sure
Great almighty Lord
The King of all living things
Return with Your mighty sword
Jesus, be my King of Kings
Jesus, be my offering

## "Don't Cry"

Don't cry little girl
Don't cry to the crowd

Remember what you heard
Remember what He said

Do this, not that
Do what is good

Thank you, my dear
Thanks with no fear

# Kitten

Which way did that cat go
Which way did he throw

Chase the yarn he did
Chase the yarn over here

Drop that food in your plate
Drop that food out of state

Thanks for being a friend
Thanks again, Nappy-Chin

## "Friend"

I give my heart to thee
I give my soul to my love
God come down to me
Or meet me in the sky
My love, my Lord
My Lord of all
Yes indeed You are my heart
Yes, my Lord, You are my soul
I wonder how far I must go
I love You so
Now it's done; I must go

## "Selma"

Which of us is perfect
Which of us is pragmatic

Just a little while and we'll see
Just a little while and we'll be

Turned away from our hopes
Turned away from our thoughts

Stand will we, my Lord
Stand with God's sword

Righteousness is what we want
Righteousness is in our thoughts

Lord, go before us this day
Lord, go before our hopes and stay

# Anniversary

It's that time again
It's that time to grin

Love has brought us full circle
Love has brought us full to purple

Royalty is the color of the day
Royalty is the color to stay

Jesus is the One we praise
Jesus is the one; He saves

Now hold me so close
Now hold our hearts with joy

Blessed on our day
Blessed on the way

Sat 4TH July 2020
3:03 pm

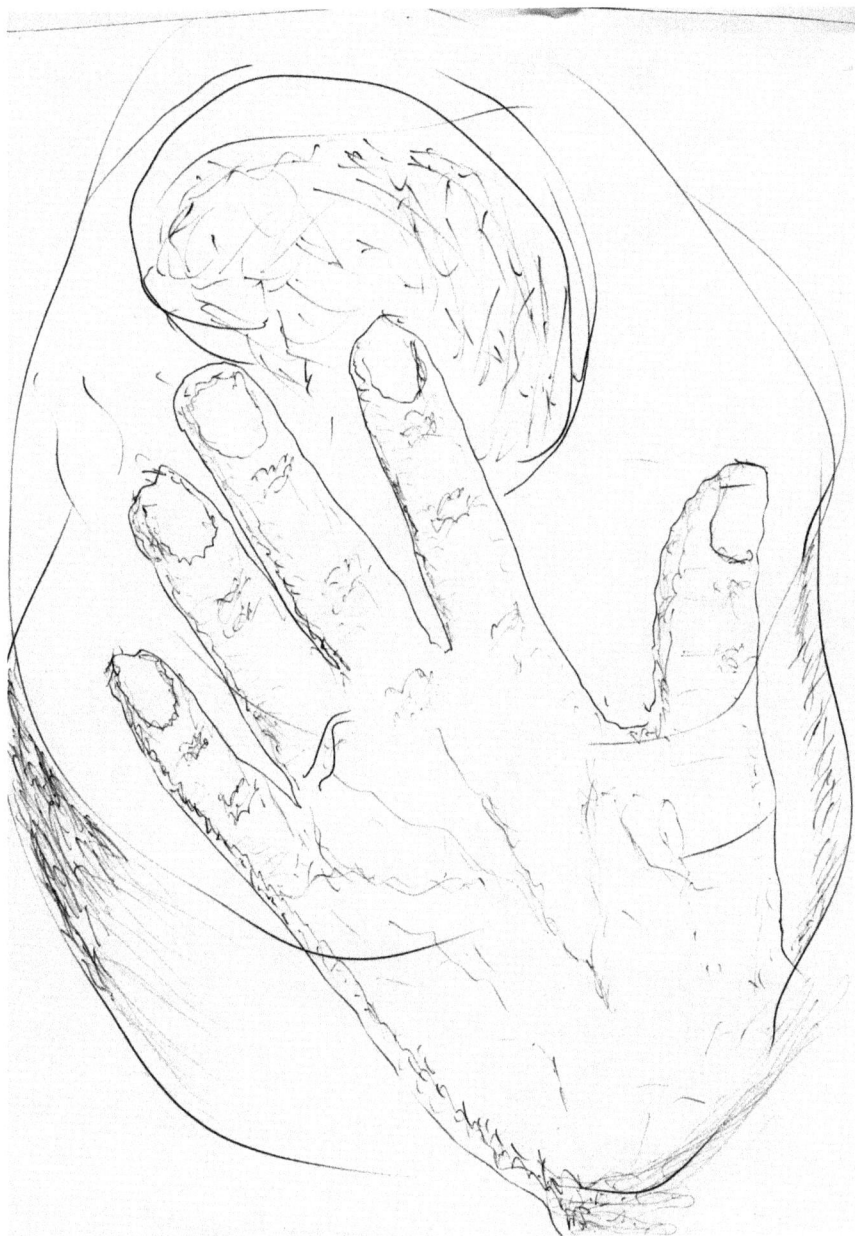

www.ingramcontent.com/pod-product-compliance
Lightning Source LLC
Chambersburg PA
CBHW021122020426
42331CB00004B/580